ADELAIDE

Aboriginal tribes lived in South Australia before the coming of Europeans.

In early 1802, Captain Matthew Flinders in HMS *Investigator* surveyed Port Lincoln and Spencer Gulf, sighted Mount Lofty from Kangaroo Head on Kangaroo Island, and explored Gulf St Vincent. After three decades in which sealers were the main visitors to its coasts, the province of South Australia was founded using Edward Gibbon Wakefield's theory that colonial land should be sold at a "sufficient price" to finance migration of Britain's excess population. In October 1835 the South Australian Company was formed. Colonel William Light was appointed Surveyor-General and Captain John Hindmarsh Governor. The Governor and some 170 passengers arrived at Holdfast Bay (Glenelg) on 28 December 1836 in HMS *Buffalo*. After extensive exploration, Light decided on Adelaide's site and confirmed his choice despite Hindmarsh's objections.

Under the efficient Governor George Grey (1841–45), the colony's finances improved dramatically from the 1840s with the exploitation of silver-lead and copper. While mining brought spectacular wealth, the profits from wheat, wool and wine grew steadily. Today South Australia's chief exports are still wool, grain, wine and minerals.

Many of the early European settlers were religious nonconformists, and the colony was built without convict labour. The State has a history of political and social innovation: in 1894 it was the first Australian colony to introduce votes for women, and it was the first to appoint an Aborigine, and, later, a woman as State Governor. Multiculturalism was welcomed and artistic development and diversity encouraged, helping to create the "Festival State".

Although South Australia is the driest State, its seas abound in fish and crustaceans. In the south's Mediterranean climate, where most of the population lives, more than half of Australia's wine is produced. Olive oil production, too, is expanding. The fertile lands bordering the River Murray yield rich produce.

Beyond Adelaide, the landscape varies from the craggy peaks of the Flinders Ranges to the grand coasts of Eyre Peninsula and rolling dunes of the Simpson Desert in the arid north-east. South Australia is a State of exciting contrasts.

Above: *Adelaide's General Post Office stands in King William Street beside Victoria Square.* **Bottom from left to right:** *The Adelaide Casino and Railway Station, North Terrace; Old Parliament House, built in 1855, is now the State History Centre; the present Parliament House was built with Kapunda marble.*

Above: *The memorial in Pennington Gardens to those who died in World War I. St Peter's Cathedral, North Adelaide, in the background, stands on the corner of Pennington Terrace and King William Street.*

ADELAIDE – DESIGNED FOR SAFETY AND GRACE

Adelaide city centre was laid out according to Surveyor-General William Light's plan, on a simple grid pattern around five open squares. The site, of about two and a half square kilometres, surmounted a gentle rise to the west and north, chosen for defensive purposes, and had a stepped boundary on the east facing the hills. The broad outer and central streets, such as North Terrace and King William Street, lend grace and space to the city. North of the city itself, beyond the lake formed by the damming of the River Torrens, is gracious North Adelaide, centred on Wellington Square. The two sections of Adelaide are separated and surrounded by parklands, in which are found the Botanic Gardens, the Zoological Gardens, other extensive and well-kept garden areas, the famed Adelaide Oval, Victoria Park Racecourse, the Municipal Golf Course and many other recreational areas.

A GARDEN CITY

In the nation's driest State, Adelaide has extensive public gardens for the delight of citizens and visitors alike. Native and exotic plants vie for the viewer's eye, with colourful annuals and perennials among the shady trees and spreading lawns.

Top: *The landscaped banks of the River Torrens (left) and the parklands provide recreational areas in the city.*
Above: *Beyond the Rotunda in Elder Park lie the Festival Centre and the Central Business District.*
Facing page: *The Palm House in the Botanic Gardens was restored in 1995 to its nineteenth-century glory.*

Top: *A busker among the shoppers in Rundle Mall.* **Above, left to right:** *Regent Arcade, one of many retail arcades in the city; The Slide, by John Dowie, in Rundle Mall.*

A CITY FOR PEOPLE

The retail shopping areas in Adelaide revolve around two precincts – Rundle Mall and the Central Market.

In the north-eastern corner of the city the Mall and its numerous arcades boast the large department stores and many specialist shops.

The Central Market, between Grote and Gouger Streets, is indeed central and easily accessible by foot or free bus. It is a retail fresh food market, displaying fruit and vegetables, smallgoods, meat, fish and bread in colourful profusion. Extending the food theme are various restaurants, delicatessens and cafés in Gouger Street. Asian, European and eclectic Australian menus vie in a busy trade.

The Central Market has served the people of Adelaide for more than a century, and is more popular today than its far-sighted planners could ever have dreamed.

Above: *A cheerful vendor beside his well-stocked Central Market stall.* **Below:** *In Rundle Mall, the city's oldest surviving retail arcade, Adelaide Arcade (left), is a stately reminder of the Victorian Period; three of the four very popular bronze pigs (right) that make up* A Day Out *by Marguerite Derricourt.*

THE RIVER TORRENS

In the first years of settlement, the people of Adelaide drew their water from the River Torrens, then an insignificant seasonal stream. The river was dammed in 1881 and its banks have undergone extensive landscaping since then. Today, the river is regulated by weirs to form Torrens Lake, which divides Adelaide from North Adelaide. The Victoria, Adelaide, Albert and Hackney Bridges span the river within the city boundaries. A footbridge provides a route from the University of Adelaide to its sports grounds across the river. The Torrens is used for sport and recreation, and pedal boats can be hired near the Adelaide and Victoria Bridges. The River Torrens Linear Park is a remarkable concept: it will follow the banks of the river from the hills to the sea, offering many recreational opportunities. The park's construction involves the removal of the more invasive exotic plant species and their replacement with some of the original native species.

Previous pages: *An aerial view of Adelaide city and the River Torrens with the Festival Centre and Convention Centre at centre and Adelaide Oval at bottom right.* **Facing page:** *The Festival Centre.* **Above:** *The excursion launch Popeye on Torrens Lake.*

Top: *Visitors walk through the foyer of the the South Australian Musuem.*
Above: *The Museum's impressive facade illuminated against the twilight sky.*

THE SOUTH AUSTRALIAN MUSEUM

Situated on North Terrace, the South Australian Museum is Adelaide's most popular cultural institution, and is noted for its Australian Aboriginal collections and cultural history exhibits. Its twin structure, the Mortlock Library, was refurbished using the old decorating crafts of graining and marbling to simulate wood and marble surfaces. Nearby stand the Art Gallery of South Australia and the State Library.

Top, left to right: *The South African War Memorial outside Government House on the corner of North Terrace and King William Street; the National Soldiers' War Memorial on the corner of North Terrace and Kintore Avenue showing a student, a farmer and a young girl watched over by an armed angel representing the Spirit of Duty.* **Above, left to right:** *The statue of Scots poet Robert Burns; a symbolic figure looks down from the plinth of the statue of King Edward VII in Prince Henry Gardens.*

NORTH TERRACE

The northern side of the gracious boulevard of North Terrace is lined with public buildings of dignity and beauty, set in lawns and gardens, with many trees for shade in Adelaide's hot summers. The buildings include libraries, museums, universities, administrative buildings and the Royal Adelaide Hospital. It is also home to a wealth of statues and monuments. Set in the footpath are tablets commemorating people who have given notable service to the State.

Above: *Carclew Youth Arts Centre on Montefiore Hill, North Adelaide, was the home of the Bonython family from 1908 to 1965. The house was built in 1897 on the site of James Chambers' house, from where John McDouall Stuart set off to cross Australia from south to north in 1861.* **Below:** *The gates of the Botanic Gardens came from London in 1880.*

Above: *The Mitchell Building, Adelaide University, North Terrace.*

COLONEL LIGHT'S LEGACY

Light prepared a coloured map of Adelaide and noted "the dark green around the town I proposed to the Resident Commissioner to be reserved as Park Lands". This foresight was to play a large part in making Adelaide the delightful green-girdled city it is today. The green belt and the broad streets and boulevards add to its beauty, and make a fine setting for the lovely houses, government offices and municipal buildings built in the architectural style of the Victorian era.

In South Australia the people have held their heritage dear, providing the funds and interest to make sure that their public buildings are sensitively updated to make way for the power supplies and amenities demanded by twenty-first century life and work, while ensuring that the buildings keep their grace and integrity.

Adelaide stands by Gulf St Vincent, and is bounded on the east by the Mount Lofty Ranges. There is something in this gracious city to please everyone – the Festival, the casino, museums, galleries, restaurants and cafés, markets and boutiques. Adelaide is an alluring gateway to South Australia.

NAUTICAL HISTORY

Although Kangaroo Island had already been visited by sealers, whalers and even settlers, the official establishment of settlement came with the arrival of Captain John Hindmarsh at Holdfast Bay (Glenelg) on 28 December 1836 in HMS *Buffalo*. As initial Governor, Hindmarsh proclaimed the establishment of the Colony of South Australia to his some 170 pioneering passengers. Port Adelaide, then known as Port Misery because of mud, mangroves and biting insects, was inadequate for larger vessels, which had to anchor in Holdfast Bay and land passengers and goods through the shallows at Glenelg. Later on, jetties were built at various locations to facilitate maritime trade, the Port River was dredged and wharf facilities were constructed, while the Outer Harbour was formed by dredging a channel and building a breakwater. Port Adelaide is home to the Port Dock Station Museum, a Maritime Museum and a translocated lighthouse in working order.

Above, left to right: *This replica of HMS Buffalo lies in Patawalonga Boat Haven, Adelphi Terrace, Glenelg.*
Facing page: *Lighthouse and historic buildings at Queen's Wharf, Port Adelaide.*

Above: *The foreshore at Glenelg, and the Glenelg Jetty stretching in to Gulf St Vincent.* **Below:** *The view across the foreshore reserve where lies the anchor of the sailing ship Trottman, along Jetty Road, Glenelg. On the left are the council chambers and information centre; on the right the Stamford Grand Hotel.*

Above: *Glenelg Jetty stretches into Gulf St Vincent.*

GLENELG

The most frequented of Adelaide's many safe, white sandy beaches is Glenelg. Here on 28 December each year, celebrations are held to commemorate the proclamation of the colony in 1836. The highlight is a famous professional foot race, the Bay Sheffield. Glenelg offers opportunities for fishing for the renowned King George Whiting or the local favourite, Tommy Ruffs, swimming and yachting. Restaurants and cafés, shops and hotels cater for the more relaxed. The local area boasts many sporting teams, prominent among which are cricket, Australian football, bowls, lacrosse and croquet. Historic buildings and monuments abound, alongside fine examples of the domestic architecture of the Victorian era. Glenelg is in easy reach of Adelaide's domestic and international air terminals, which has no doubt added to its popularity with travellers.

Above: *Rotunda and St Andrews Uniting Church in Strathalbyn, south-east of Adelaide, a service town for farming areas and the burgeoning Langhorne Creek grape-growing industry.* **Below, left to right:** *The heritage-listed Old Mill at Hahndorf, now guest accommodation, function rooms and restaurant; the famous German Arms, Hahndorf.*

THE ADELAIDE HILLS

The Adelaide Hills is a name loosely applied to part of the Mount Lofty Ranges, the southern end of the Barossa Ranges and hilly parts of northern Fleurieu Peninsula. Green and fertile, they attracted many early settlers who established orchards, market gardens, and dairy and grain farms. Typical of the many small towns is Hahndorf, settled in 1839 by Germans seeking religious freedom and land. They named their town in honour of their captain, who brought them safely to landfall and helped select their farmland. Nearby is Lobethal (German for Valley of Praise). The German heritage is zealously preserved, and the annual Schuetzenfest and Hahndorf Founders Day are celebrated among well-maintained traditional German-style buildings. In more recent times, the cool climate of the Adelaide Hills has attracted makers of premium wines.

Top: *Plump sheep and sturdy vines flourish in the Adelaide Hills.* **Above:** *The traditional sign for the Old Hahndorf Village Market cannot help but catch the visitor's eye.*

Facing page: *A fine surf beach at Pennington Bay in Kangaroo Island's south-east.* **Top:** *Admirals Arch at Cape de Couedic in the island's south-west.* **Above, left to right:** *An Australian Sea-lion at Seal Bay Conservation Park on the south coast; a pair from about 700 Australian Sea-lions that congregate at Seal Bay.*

KANGAROO ISLAND

Kangaroo Island, at about 160 kilometres long and 60 kilometres wide at its broadest, is Australia's third largest island. It was visited by Matthew Flinders in 1802. In the following year, the French visited and American sealers stayed at American River for four months, during which time they built the first boat made in the State, the *Independence*. The barque *Duke of York* landed the island's first British colonists at Nepean Bay on the north coast on 27 July 1836, soon to be joined by other ships. The island is now popular with tourists and holidaymakers, drawn by the flora and fauna, fishing, boating and diving. The island is a short flight from Adelaide, and there are frequent ferries between Cape Jervis on the mainland and Kingscote and Penneshaw. With improved transport, Kangaroo Island producers are now earning fame as makers of fine foods and wines.

REMARKABLE ROCKS

On the dome of Kirkpatrick Point, to the east of Cape de Couedic, stands the group of huge, weather-sculpted rocks known as Remarkable Rocks. Their sides have been undercut by caverns thought to have been caused by the crystallisation of salts within the structure of the rock itself. Their rich reds are the natural colour of ironstone: lichens form contrasting streaks of orange and grey-green. The dwarfed vegetation is indicative of the harsh weather and sparse soils of the exposed south-west of Kangaroo Island.

Above and facing page: *The extraordinary pits and melon holes weathered in the granite of the Remarkable Rocks, Kangaroo Island, emphasise the power and persistence of wind, water and temperature.*

Above: *The "cultural capital" of the Barossa Valley, Tanunda, nestles beside the Barossa Ranges, surrounded in this summer scene by brown farm paddocks and rich green vineyards.*
Bottom: *Looking across the vineyards to the Barossa Ranges, with Little Kaiser Stuhl and Kaiser Stuhl at centre.*

Top: *Oak storage for maturing wines.* **Above, left to right:** *The Cellar Door at Peter Lehmann Winery, Tanunda, serves also as an art gallery; Chateau Tanunda winery in Tanunda.*

A WORLD OF WINEMAKING

The Barossa Valley, some 75 kilometres north-east of Adelaide, enjoys a Mediterranean climate, with cool rainy winters and warm to hot summers. Grape vines flourish in this ambience. Early autumn brings the start of the harvest each year, when grapes are picked, carted to the weighbridges and crushed around the clock for weeks. The excellent vintages produced in the Barossa Valley ensure that South Australian wines are valued for their quality throughout the world. Other areas of the State, notably the Clare Valley, the Riverland, the Adelaide Hills, the Southern Vales, Langhorne Creek, Coonawarra, Padtheway and the Limestone Coast contribute richly to this fine reputation. Wine is a major South Australian export. Amateur winemaking is popular, and each year the national wine and beer contest sees keen competition for trophies and medals.

THE BAROSSA VALLEY

In the early 1840s settlers from Silesia, Prussia and Brandenburg entered the Barossa Valley, a fertile area stretching north from a point about 55 kilometres north-east of Adelaide. They came to escape religious persecution and economic oppression, and they cultivated their new land with meticulous care. Today the Barossa is a region of flourishing vineyards and numerous wineries. Picturesque towns and villages such as Greenock, Nuriootpa, Angaston, Tanunda, Bethany and Lyndoch preserve much of the German heritage. Brass bands abound, as do choirs. As well as the jovial Kaffeeabend, more formal festivities are held, such as the Barossa Classic Gourmet Weekend and the Barossa Music Festival. Every second year the Barossa Vintage Festival is held in April, a seven-day enthusiastic harvest thanksgiving. The food of the Barossa reflects the people's German origins, through wurst and dill pickles to rich pastries, and a local version of German, Barossa Deutsch, is still spoken.

Top, left to right: *A grape picker at work; red grapes maturing.*
Bottom: *An elegant nineteenth-century house, with its characteristic verandahs and chimneys, sits amid old vines.*

The buildings of the Barossa Valley are largely made from stone – bluestone, sandstone or ironstone, with marble often present for decorative purposes. A large proportion, especially of public buildings, are monuments to the crafts and reliability of their nineteenth-century builders. A typical Barossa Valley town has a number of churches, the Lutheran ones with characteristic tall spires stretching toward the heavens. More modern structures often display the same solidity of construction and purpose. Other crafts flourish too: smithing, weaving, pottery, painting, sculpture and leathercraft. These may be viewed in business premises and museums.

Top: *A row of elegant old buildings display the decorative and long-lasting work of skilled stonemasons.*
Above, left to right: *Craft and antiques displayed in Tanunda; the cellar door at Chateau Yaldara.*

Top: *The Telegraph Station Gallery, Victor Harbor.*   **Above, left to right:** *The broad footpaths and wide verandahs reveal Victor Harbor's nineteenth-century origins; a bank building stands impressively on a corner.*
Facing page: *The old horse tram still carries passengers from Victor Harbor to Granite Island.*

VICTOR HARBOR

Victor Harbor, a little over 80 kilometres south of Adelaide, was once a major port for the River Murray trade and is now a leading tourist and retirement destination. The area was first settled in 1837, and was one of a number of seashore sites for the capital of South Australia favoured by Governor John Hindmarsh, a naval officer. Originally known as Alexandra, it was gazetted as Victor Harbor, and that unusual spelling is retained. The railway linking Victor Harbor with the river port of Goolwa was extended to join the Adelaide railway system, but is now used only for excursion trains, usually steam driven. The Cockle Train offers a scenic ride between Victor Harbor and Goolwa. A horse-drawn tram plies along a kilometre of causeway between Victor Harbor and Granite Island.

Above: *The River Murray near the town of Nildottie.* **Below, left to right:** *An Australian Pelican on the Coorong, which runs south-east from the mouth of the Murray and is famed for its birdlife; a shrimp fisherman on Lake Alexandrina, at the river mouth.*

THE RIVER MURRAY

For irrigation along its banks and for pipeline distribution to Adelaide, Whyalla and many other centres, the water of the River Murray is the lifeblood of the State of South Australia. Irrigation was begun in 1887. It was made possible by a series of weirs with locks to facilitate boat use. This reduced seasonal variation in river levels. The first section of the river after it enters South Australia is called the Riverland, and is renowned for citrus and stone fruit orchards and vineyards. The towns of Renmark, Barmera, Loxton, Berri and Waikerie are centres for the distribution and processing of the products of the irrigation blocks. Typical manufacture includes dried fruit production, juice extraction and winemaking. After the Murray makes its abrupt turn southward at Morgan, the area is known as the Murraylands, and dairying and recreation are more important uses of the river's waters. On both sections of the river, large pleasure boats and smaller self-drive houseboats are very popular with vacationers. Fishing is common from shore and boats. Problems have resulted from the regulation of the waters of the river: the more serious is the rise of salinity levels, but worries also arise from the interruption to the natural flow of the River Murray, causing difficulties in keeping a channel open to allow an outflow into the sea.

Above: *Paddlewheelers still ply the Murray, taking holidaymakers for a leisurely trip out of time. But it was different when the river was the only path for goods to travel, and the riverboats held furious races to carry the first of the wool-clip to market.*

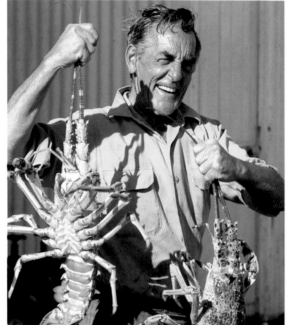

Top: *Fishing is a common occupation in Kingston, Robe, Beachport and Port MacDonnell.* **Above, left to right:** *A Kingston crayfisher displays his catch; Cape Northumberland at Port MacDonnell, with its very necessary lighthouse in the background.*

THE SOUTH-EAST

This area is better watered than most of South Australia, and is blessed with a reliable subterranean water resource. Grain farming, grazing, grape growing, fishing and softwood forestry are the bases of the region's prosperity. The most important centre is Mount Gambier, the "capital" of the South-East, but Millicent, Naracoorte, Bordertown and Keith are significant service towns. Penola serves the internationally respected premium grape-growing district of Coonawarra. The area's fertility arose from the presence of a number of long-extinct volcanoes. Many of the craters now contain lakes, the most famous of which is the Blue Lake at Mount Gambier. Three kilometres in circumference and very deep, it changes colour from dull grey to deep blue in November. The limestone beneath the surface houses many spectacular caves.

Above: *Substantial Australian regional cities usually have at least one spacious and dignified hotel where out-of-town landholders may stay in comfort: this one is in Mount Gambier.*
Below, left to right: *Visitors wonder at the startling blueness of the Blue Lake; rural countryside near Mount Gambier.*

Top: *The ruins of Lake Harry homestead on the Birdsville Track, north-east South Australia.*
Above: *Alfrinck carves talc stone in his studio at Lyndhurst in the north-east.*

OUTBACK SOUTH AUSTRALIA

The Outback of South Australia is dry, hot, dusty and sparsely vegetated. Stock is counted not in beasts per hectare, but in number of square kilometres per beast. Towns and homesteads are far apart; often the only link is by a sandy or rocky track. It takes special people to make a living here, but they do. Making the best of what you have is one of the keys to survival in this arid country, which occupies 80 per cent of the State's area, but is home to less than half a per cent of the population. The friendly people who live here have compensation in the stark beauty of the land and the brilliant floral carpets that follow the rare rains. The Stuart Highway is a sealed road, and the Birdsville and Strzelecki Tracks are negotiable with care. Travellers in the Outback should take sensible precautions – the unprepared have died all too often – and should treat the vulnerable environment with care.

THE GHAN RAILWAY

The Ghan railway was named after the Afghan camel-drivers whose beasts carried supplies through the Outback. It ran from Port Augusta north through South Australia to Alice Springs in the Northern Territory. Travel on the Old Ghan was often adventurous, especially if flash floods isolated the train or carried away sections of track. Once the engine driver had to shoot goats to feed his passengers. The Old Ghan line was closed in 1980. Travellers on the present Ghan follow the Adelaide–Perth track to Tarcoola and then proceed north hundreds of kilometres to the west of the old track. The line is being extended to link Darwin with Alice Springs.

Top: *An abandoned siding on the old Ghan railway.*
Above: *Tearing up the tracks of the old Ghan railway.*

THE EYRE PENINSULA

Named after Edward John Eyre, who crossed it in 1840, this peninsula produces about ten per cent of Australia's wheat crop, but retains much natural bush and offers great diversity of landscapes. Nearly half the peninsula is set aside as reserves, parks and native bushland. Its eastern coast features sandy beaches, and boat fishing, commercial and recreational, is common. The western coast becomes increasingly rugged as it approaches the head of the Great Australian Bight. Coffin Bay National Park near the south-western end of the peninsula offers especially beautiful and unspoilt coastal wilderness.

Top: *The many eastern beaches of the Eyre Peninsula are ideal for anglers.*   **Above:** *Morning light on the beach, Lincoln National Park.*   **Facing page:** *Sunset on the Southern Ocean, Coffin Bay National Park.*

Top: *Port Augusta stands at the head of Spencer Gulf.*
Above: *The Whyalla was built in Whyalla in 1941 and is displayed at Whyalla Maritime Museum.*

PORT AUGUSTA AND WHYALLA

Port Augusta stands at the most northerly navigable point of Spencer Gulf. Warm, sunny days make it a holiday destination in midwinter. Once an important port for wheat, wool and minerals, it is now a railway and industrial centre, servicing rail traffic from Perth, Adelaide, Sydney and Alice Springs. The Northern Power Station produces about 40 per cent of South Australia's power needs.

Whyalla, South Australia's largest regional city, is sometimes called the gateway to the Eyre Peninsula. Situated on the north-western shores of Spencer Gulf, it owed its development to the presence of huge deposits of iron ore in the nearby Middleback Ranges. With Port Augusta and Port Pirie it forms the "Iron Triangle" of regional heavy industry. Whyalla once held a flourishing steelworks and ship-yard. It has an excellent maritime museum.

THE WEST COAST

The West Coast, as the western shores of the Eyre Peninsula are known, has some wonderful coastal scenery. A particular attraction is the arrival of the Southern Right Whales between July and October each year, as they migrate to breed. Recreational boat fishing is popular, and important commercial fisheries include the harvesting of Abalone, Southern Bluefin Tuna and King George Whiting.

Top, left to right: *A splendid beach in Coffin Bay National Park; Lincoln National Park is just south of Port Lincoln.*
Above: *Cape Carnot, south-west of Port Lincoln, is an important fishing and tourist town near the southern end of the Eyre Peninsula. The coastline here is known for its rugged grandeur.*

Above: *Mulga trees at sunset on the eastern Nullarbor Plain.* **Below, left to right:** *A salt lake in Nullarbor National Park; an intrepid cyclist crossing the Nullarbor on the way to Perth; bluebush and other drought-resistant plants survive on the arid plain.*

Top, left to right: *Sheer sea cliffs over the Great Australian Bight; fettlers' camp on the Nullarbor.*
Above, left to right: *Children from Cook Primary School enjoy a music lesson on the Nullarbor Plain; the Southern Hairy-nosed Wombat, faunal symbol of South Australia, lives in burrows on the Nullarbor Plain.*

THE NULLARBOR PLAIN

The word "Nullarbor" literally means "no tree", but some stunted trees manage to survive on this vast arid plain, and the diversity of smaller plants is amazing. Once this area lay under the sea. Earth movements pushed it upwards to form an expanse of limestone, beneath whose surface are extensive cave systems. The limestone ends at the Great Australian Bight in precipitous cliffs. The plain has interesting wildlife: like many other arid-country creatures, the Southern Hairy-nosed Wombat escapes the heat of the day by living in a burrow. At night it is very vulnerable on roads as it is slow-moving, and motorists should take care to avoid it. The Indian–Pacific train crosses the Nullarbor. Tiny settlements named after former Prime Ministers are scattered along it, housing track maintenance crews and their families.

Top: *The delicate flowers of this Ptilotus species are in strong contrast to the harsh background of the Painted Desert.*
Above, left to right: *The Central Netted Dragon survives in dry, sandy areas; Galahs, the Jokers of the Bush.*

THE NORTHERN DESERTS

A group of extensive national parks and reserves guards the fragile ecology of South Australia's arid northern areas. The Simpson Desert Regional Reserve and Simpson Desert Conservation Park, west of the Birdsville Track and extending into Queensland and the Northern Territory, include a seemingly endless series of red sand dunes, gibber plains, salt lakes, spinifex grass and gidgee woodlands. After a rare fall of rain, the desert plants will put out leaves, flower spectacularly and set seeds that can survive long periods of drought. Following heavy falls, standing water seems to be covered almost overnight by flocks of birds.